Black Libertarianism
in the Blue State

Joshua FLYNN

BLACK LIBERTARIANISM IN THE BLUE STATE

Amazon Digital Services, LLC

Table of Contents

About the Author

Joshua Flynn is a businessman and a politician from Austin, a neighborhood in the Westside of Chicago, in Cook County. He is a political candidate, running for the Illinois State House for the 2020 election against Camille Lilly.

Before endeavoring himself into the political realm, Joshua owned two businesses, one in the insurance industry and the other in the truck driving industry. He is currently pursuing his college degree at Jarvis Christian College while campaigning full-time.

Joshua is a husband and a father of three children. In addition to be a businessman and a politician, he is also a sharecropper like his parents were. He owns a farm. Joshua is one of the very few black politicians who runs for office on a libertarian ticket. Furthermore, he is the recipient of the Libertarian Leadership Award. He was awarded that prize on March 14, 2020 by the Libertarian Party of Illinois at the State Convention. Josh has been giving many interviews on local radio channels and various libertarian media outlets to discuss his campaign and political platform. *Black Libertarianism in the Blue State* is Josh's first published works.

Acknowledgements

The completion of this project was long one and it could have not been done without the participation of certain people in the process. In this acknowledgment section, I would like to thank three groups.

First, I would like to thank my wife, Ramona, and my two wonderful children, Jocelyn and E'Londre for their unconditional support in my political journey. Running for office is not an easy decision to make. My wife has always supported me in this endeavor and has always believed in my ambition. She did play a great role in the process of the completion of this book.

Second, I would like to thank my campaign team. Each member of my team has played a diligent role in providing substantive insights to the development of the ideas of this book. Each of their insights has been a mental challenge in order to write a good book. It helped me grow and becoming a better person throughout the campaign trail.

Lastly, I would like to thank the Libertarian Party of Illinois as well as that of Chicago for accepting me for who I am and for my political convictions. I found in them my political family and I am very grateful that they changed my life for the better.

Preface

Black Libertarianism in the Blue State is an unusual book title. But it says it all. The State of Illinois is a "blue" state in political terms. The conventional political wisdom in Illinois is that an individual, especially one of color, ought to be a liberal. Of course, in the United States, the word "liberal" has lost its original sense and purpose. Etymologically, the word "liberal" means an ideology that promotes the freedom of the individual in a civil society, and the restriction of political authority over the citizenry. In other words, liberalism advocates for limited government and the individual rights of the citizen in a civil society. However, this fundamental definition has changed through the course of history. Today, in the United States, liberalism no longer mean limited government and expansion of individual

xiii

rights, but expansion of political power and the reduction of individual liberties. This is the ideology that the Democratic Party has been advocating for since its inception. And this has become the mainstream ideology that dominates Illinois politics.

Furthermore, today in the United States, over two-third of the African American population votes for the Democratic Party. It is expected by our society that a black person must and shall be a liberal, a progressive, a socialist, and a left-wing activist. In other words, a Black person is expected to vote Democrat even if the policies suggested by the Democratic Party do not benefit Black people overall. Unsurprisingly, my political opponent for this forthcoming election, Camille Lilly, is an African American and a Democrat.

In the State of Illinois, I am the exception to the rule. I become the heterodoxy trend to mainstream politics. When a Black person expresses her preference for private property, free market economics, self-ownership, individual liberties, and personal responsibility; this person is automatically classified by his peers and fellowmen as a "coon"; "Uncle Tom"; and "Oreo Cookie"; or a "traitor." I find this childish and tribalistic attitude ironic. I did not know that promoting liberty and the emancipation of the individual meant that it is betraying the cause of Black people. I did not know that being patronized by the government was more important than being free. Evidently, my assertions here are sarcastic. In fact, it is irrational to me that instead of supporting liberty, most of my Black fellowmen are supporting the power of the state over their own lives. Whether it consciously or unconsciously, each vote they cast for the Democratic Party at every election cycle, is a request and a boon for the state to patronize them. It is an opportunity once again for the Democratic Party to mock us, to make their point that Black people cannot be self-reliant. Make no mistake, I used to be a Democrat myself. I used to vote Democrat every election cycle since I turned 18, without even understanding what was at stake. I used to vote Democrat simply out of conventional wisdom. I used to vote Democrat because that was the trend to follow as a Black person if you want to fit in. I used to vote Democrat until I finally became intellectually, politically, and ideologically conscientious.

I write this book with one purpose: to propose an alternative viewpoint to the voter. I believe that the voter should be exposed to other views than what he is told by the local liberal media on a daily basis. Before casting his or her vote this November; I want the voter to read and understand my viewpoint; to comprehend why I believe in what I believe. I want the voter to give a chance to open-mindedness. Lastly, I want the voter to encounter libertarianism. Libertarianism, to me is the true movement of equality, a movement wherein we are all equal in our pursuit for freedom. I seek to impact the reader and the voter with my writings. I hope that this book will complete its task and change the reader and voter's perspectives of politics.

This book is divided into two parts. The first part of the book is more autobiographical. In fact, it emphasizes on the major events of my life, from my birth until my intellectual awakening. The second part is more of a political analysis. It elaborates on the major elements of my platform.

Part One
THE MAN

CHAPTER ONE

HUMBLE CHILDHOOD

It was a snowy day on this day of December 28, 1986. My mother was at Sinai Hospital giving birth to me. I can surely imagine that it was a painful childbirth. I am not sure if this is necessarily true, but I heard that if a child was born out of a painful childbirth, it usually means that this child was meant to have a brilliant career in his life. In other words, the pain that a mother endures while bearing a child during pregnancy worth the sacrifice of birthing him. I will surely need some empirical evidence in order to actually believe in it but as I reflect on my career, and how I have come this far, I must admit that this tale could be possibly true. I have never thought one day that I would have accomplished what I have accomplished in my life at thirty-four years old. The grace of God is what has led me here.

What I have accomplished in my life humbles me more because I come from a conventional African American middle-class family. My mother was a sharecropper from Brandon, Mississippi, and my father was also a sharecropper from Capleville, Tennessee. None of my parents was wealthy. They worked hard all their lives in order to be able to feed a family of twelve children of whom I was the youngest. My parents were surely not wealthy in terms of material possessions, but they were wealthy in terms of education, moral values, and civic duties. The education that I have today, the lessons of life that I learned throughout my existence; I owe it to my parents. They did not only teach me how to be a man, they also taught me how to respect the individual regardless of his skin color, religious values, or moral principles. I guess, this were my very first signals as a prospective libertarian.

My father was a member of the Church of God in Christ Bishop on the Westside of Chicago. I can remember as if it was yesterday, how he would always make me go to church even during times that I did not feel like it. My old man never missed a day of church even when he was sick, unless the malady was severe or chronicle. He was utterly dedicated to the Church and to give his life to Christ. In fact, my father is the principal engine of my religious faith. I can remember when he used to tell me: *"No matter how difficult a situation is, or how your condition could be, always remember that God is always with you! Always keep the faith, and never give up! Sooner or later, your condition will improve."* Indeed, my old man was right. His advices were crucial for my adult life. He could be tough sometimes, but he was tough for the right reasons. Evidently, as a child, I did not grasp why he would be tough on me. I used to wrongly interpret his deeds towards me. But today, I fully understand that all of his deeds were simply meant to pave the way for my success.

Obedience and respect were the core values that my father has conveyed and inculcated in each of my siblings and myself, of course. And I have passed on those same principles to my children as well. My father deeply insisted on the need for obedience because obedience is the element that maintains a household in order and establishes stability. My siblings and I never challenged the authority of my father because we believed that his judgement was right. Whatever he decided, we believed that he made such decisions for a good reason. Moreover, obedience itself is a fundamental characteristic of Black culture. When we observe today the Black family unit, we clearly see that it has been decimated by the liberal policies of the welfare state. More than two-third of Black families are fatherless, and this fatherlessness has led to a significant increase of crime rate in our community. I realize how my father used obedience as a tool to ensure the unity and stability of our family. Today, thanks to his education, I am also a married man, with a wonderful wife, and I fully assume my role as father, and I make sure that my children lack nothing. Besides being a sharecropper, my father also worked for thirty-eight years for Imperial Eastman as a manufacturing engineer. He was a diligent and industrious worker. Work and family have been his whole life until he recently passed away. Even in his old days, he kept working at the farm that he owned. For my father, work was a way for him to live.

My mother was not entirely different from my father. She was a tough black woman. Her greatest asset in life was her drive to succeed. She adamantly believed that one will ultimately succeed if he has the drive for it regardless on the endeavor that he or she might pursue. For her, ambition and commitment were the core elements of success on earth. For her, ambition was necessary condition to become successful but not sufficient condition. Commitment is the sufficient element to achieve success. I could not agree more with my mother's philosophy. She strongly believed in self-reliance. She was convinced that man should rely on no one else but himself and grace of God in order to experience the wonders of life. Once again, my old lady was not wrong. She was a business owner in the 1960s and 1970s. She owned two pubs on the Westside as well as real estate properties. It was purely and simply amazing to see a black woman accomplishing those things in a country that has been for generations, detrimental to us. But my mother's accomplishments were the ultimate proof that success is color-blinded. Success is not something that is solely attributed to white people or to Jewish people. It is something that is attributed to anyone who is self-reliant, regardless of what his or her cultural, racial, sexual, and religious background may be.

My mother was accomplishing these things in the 1960s when Blacks barely obtained the civil rights, and in the 1970s when Nixon enforced his War on Drugs policies, which have profoundly yet perniciously affected the Black community. If my mother was a single mother, I am convinced that she would have not achieved what she has achieved. Make no mistake, it does not mean that a single mother is necessarily doomed to remain poor; of course not, but it is surely more difficult to be economically self-sufficient when you are a single mother with many children to take care of.

What strikes me the most about my parents is their resilience. Despite their limited level of education, they managed to fulfill the American Dream with the meager means they had. It is important to reiterate that my parents had a limited access to resources and yet managed to become self-sufficient while in our generation, we have an unlimited access to resources, but people are still complaining that they are struggling and cannot be self-sufficient.

I was not particularly a great student throughout my academic career. In fact, I did not really care much for school at the time. Not because school was boring but because I experienced great difficulties learning at the same pace as other students. I attended Jackie

Robinson Elementary School and graduated from it 2001. I must admit that I was a slow learner. I did not and never have any mental deficiency; I was just slow in grasping concepts that others were already comprehending, and it used to frustrate me. I had to redouble my efforts just to be on the same level as other students. Mathematics was particularly a delicate subject for me. Subsequently to my elementary school graduation, I moved on to secondary education and graduated in 2005. A year after graduating from high school, I married the love of my life, Ramona. I was only twenty years old.

What I can perfectly ascertain, is that I come from a family that had nothing but gave me everything. If my parents did not stay together, if my father had left the house and my mother have had several children with different men; I ,then, would have had ended up like the way young Black men are portrayed today; as purposeless, making bad decisions, committing crimes, and I would certainly have ended up in prison. I am adamantly convinced that the secret to the mental balance of my childhood is rooted in the fact that my parents stayed together to raise my siblings and me as a family unit.

It is undeniably clear that my father was the figurehead of the house, this authoritative figure who ensured that every single one of his children received the proper discipline to become successful in life. It is hard to become successful in life without proper guidance. Most of the Black kids who are filling out the prisons, are in prison not because they are stupid or not ambitious; but they are in prison because they did not have an authoritative figure in the house to discipline them and to guide them. They are in prison because they lack opportunities. The lack of opportunities they have is due to a lack of parental guidance. How can we expect a child to become a real man if he is only raised by his mother who has to work two or three jobs just to meet ends need? It does not mean that every single black child who grew up in a single-parent household never became successful. There are some exceptions. Indeed, Walter E. Williams, for example, one my favorite economists, and my second favorite black economist after Thomas Sowell, grew up in a single-parent household. He father deserted the house when he was about three years old if I am not mistaken. His mother worked several jobs in order to put food on the table and a roof over their heads (Dr. Williams and his sister). It was tremendously difficult for him and yet, he managed to earn his PhD in economics and became a Professor of Economics. Thank Lord, I did not have to go through what Dr. Williams went through. I was able to avoid that kind of struggle thank to the unity and guidance of my parents. Without them, I do not know if I would have had the same determination as Walter E. Williams did in order to become that successful. In that very particular case, I do feel privileged.

Dr. Williams is also one of the reasons why I progressively became a libertarian. For the fact of the matter, Professor Williams has always said what my parents have taught me. To value education, to start working early in life in order to learn discipline in the professional world, to take all kind of jobs that come my way, including the jobs that I did not want to do, to avoid having kids before I were to be married, and to avoid doing drugs. It is fair to say that today, doing drugs is no longer the same issue that it used to be some thirty years ago. Back then, drugs were heavily criminalized. The criminalization of drugs was used as a tool to maintain African Americans at the bottom of the social ladder and to deprive them from accessing to economic and social opportunities. I clearly fathomed that staying out of trouble was a prerequisite to be successful, especially for a Black man living in the United States. Having a criminal record is probably one of the worst things that could happen to someone beside having cancer or an incurable disease. As we all know, if you have a criminal record, especially like a misdemeanor or felony, you are literally set to never rent an apartment or obtaining a job. You are then locked up in this social prison which is even worse than actual prison. I made sure to stay away from anything that could jeopardize my life.

Thanks to Ramona, who has always been there for me, in addition to the support of my parents, I knew that every single action I would execute, would have to be rational and toward a specific purpose. The slightest mistake could have cost me, not only my entire youth, but my whole life. Today, I am a father and a married black politician running for political office in a Blue state in order to promote the values of liberty and justice for everyone living in District 78. The education I received from my parents did definitely set me up for the future. My childhood was a humble childhood. It was a life-lesson. I am now, more than ever, ready to give back to my community and to my family.

CHAPTER TWO

BECOMING A MAN

Everyone male wants to become a man, but not every male is willing to do what men do in order to be respected as a man. I got married at twenty years old. It was in 2006. I freshly graduated from high school. Ramona and I got engaged on October 23rd, 2006. I proposed to her during the Dallas Cowboys vs New York Giants game. I perfectly remember that the Giants won 36 to 22. And six months later, we tied the knots. My wife is also a native of Westside Chicago like I am.

Most people perceive marriage as a simple relationship where if things go south, one can simply divorce the other as an unmarried couple would have just broken up.

In this century, marriage as a social institution is losing its value. For my wife and I, marriage is not a mere relationship in which one can get in when it is convenient and get out when it is no longer the case. Marriage is a full-time job on its own. It is a lifetime commitment. It is a two-way relationship in which the two parties have committed to stay together for the best and for the worst. It is a genuine sacrament. If my parents did not see marriage as a sacrament, I would have not had the education that I have. My marriage with Ramona, like every single couple on earth, has not been an easy one. Not because Ramona is a bad wife. On the contrary. It is because she is a great wife that I am still married to her. My marriage has not been an easy one because of the challenges that my wife and I had to face in life, like every couple do. She is an excellent mother. Together, we teamed up to raise our kids, and we combined the values that both of our parents have taught us, and we conveyed these values on to our children. The greatest benefit I earned from being married to Ramona is that it made me become a man.

A woman is the one who makes a man becoming a man. She will challenge you to do things that you have never dared of doing before. She will touch on your ego and you will want to prove to her that you can do it. The good thing about this is that it made me realized that there was an enormous potential locked inside me that needed it be unlocked. Ramona did always challenge me to do the right thing. She never hesitated to tell me like it is, and to keep it, as we say in urban language, "100 percent" with me. She is a straightforward, unapologetically self-reliant woman. She, sometimes, reminds me of my mother. They both have the same philosophy and attitude toward life. She is an ambition woman like my mother, she always challenged herself, she always wanted to do better than the previous version of herself. Today she is pursuing a doctorate in education at Concordia University. She never stops learning. For her, the quest of knowledge should be the primary element that must stimulate man to seek higher aims. She is an avid reader, and she is always seeking to learn new things. She will never stop to amaze me. Ramona has always wanted for me what she wanted for her. I mean by that that she sees herself in the position that I exert. I would not be surprise if she one day runs for political office. She has the intellect and the skills to do. More importantly, she constantly pushed me to give the best version of myself. She is partially the reason why I decided to run for political office. She knew that I have always cared about the welfare of my community, and that I always wanted the people of Austin to have a better living standard than what they currently have. She told me that if I wanted to make a difference, then it is my duty to serve the needs of my community the best way I possibly can. I believe that seeking political office to implement these changes in my community would be an effective method to accomplish it.

Without the unconditional support of my wife; I would have probably been a different man. Less confident, less ambitious, and less determined. She fueled the passion of serving others in me.

Being a man also means having responsibilities and facing the consequences of my actions. I got married at a relatively young age for man. Most men married much later than at twenty years of age. I was not economically self-sufficient when I got married. I was in college and I was not passionate about what I was studying. During my third year of undergraduate, I dropped out of school. I was convinced that a college education was not for me. I subsequently decided to be active in real life by either finding a job or creating one. I started my own insurance brokerage and trucking company. It was not easy to manage two businesses. I had very little sleep hours, constantly working and looking for new opportunities to grow my business. Through my two businesses, I learned a lot about communication, accounting, customer service, and built one of the best work ethics a man could possibly have. As a business owner, I realized that entrepreneurship is the best element of life that the free market can offer to a human being. Evidently, it is far from easy. I had to wake up every day around four in the morning to start work, although I was working for myself. The support of my wife during my years of entrepreneurship were unconditionally needed and truly appreciated. Ramona was my accountant. She took care of the numbers while I was bringing in new clients. It was not easy, of course, to work with my wife. We had sometimes differences of opinion and we did not always see eye-to-eye on every business issue. But having her as a business partner was intrinsically one of the best professional decisions I have ever made. Ramona and I have helped a lot of members of the community by offering them a job at our company. Every person hired at our company was an individual who was being lifted out of poverty. Thanks to a market economy, I was able to help my fellow men; not by giving him handouts but by offering him a job so that he too could be economically self-sufficient rather than relying on welfare benefits to survive. Offering a product or service to my people was my way of giving back to the community.

In a socialist economy, I could have not become a man because the state would have attempted to subsidize me. It would have tried to subsidize me by patronizing me, by telling me that I cannot achieve anything on my own because I do not know what is good for myself, that only those who rule the state know what is best for the layman. I may be a layman, but I am not an ignorant. I would have not achieved in a socialist economy what I have achieved in a market economy. A socialist economy would have not allowed me to start my own insurance company. I would have had to work for the state, and be subjected to its rules, and regulations. It would have been highly unproductive, and I would have lost my manhood because there would be a serious lack of incentives under such economy.

Incentive is what stimulates a man to achieve great things in life. The quest to do better is what keeps me going and helps me getting out of bed by five in the morning. Working endless hour to meet ends need is almost like a relentless combat until you finally make it to the top. But I believe that it is what men are supposed to do in order to survive. The human condition is doomed to provide either physical or intellectual efforts in order to survive. I fundamentally believe that hard work sets a man free. For a man to be able to eat the fruit of his own labor is unequivocally the greatest satisfaction ever. My wife and I have struggled really hard to achieve our dreams. Raising two children in my twenties was not an easy task to do. Yet I still did it, and that is thank to my wonderful wife.

Keeping the family unit together and stable was my first priority. I could have not afforded to be an absent father to my children. My children needed guidance. Today, my first child is a college student and my other child is in high school. Putting them through school was evidently not an easy task but Ramona and I did what we had to do to ensure that our children receive the best and proper education they need in order to become successful in this world.

I must admit that seeing my son succeeding at university gave me the courage to go back to university to continue my studies in order to obtain my college degree. I am currently pursuing a bachelor's degree of business administration at Jarvis Christian College and I am planning on graduating very soon. I realize that being a man is also about facing our past and assume the consequences of our actions. I have no shame for going back to school at a later time in my life. For the fact of the matter, as my wife has always believed, we never finish learning. So long as I live, I will continue to renew myself through education because the pursuit of knowledge is incontrovertibly the only resource that could be indefinitely used without it losing its value.

My father passed away in March 2013 and my mother deceased in January 2015. They were certainly the two great losses of my life. I wish they could be here to see the man I have become thanks to their education and valuable advices. My father's death has deeply affected me because the man was not only my mentor, he was my hero and my role model. He was a tough but fair father. He was righteous. He believed that the world is a corrupt place and that righteous people must rule again because righteousness to him, was the will of God. To my old man, a righteous person would be a man or a woman who seeks self-reliance, autonomy, who would care for his or her neighbors, who would respect the rights and freedom and others, and who will never infringe upon the individual liberties of man. His teachings and prayers were a life-changer for me.

One important fact that I may have forgotten to mention is that my father started community outreach since the age of five. We used to volunteer for different candidates in the city of Chicago, in state and federal campaigns as well. I believe my interest in politics has started early by spending time with my father on the campaign trail. He did deeply believe that politics is an endeavor that was meant to promulgate change for the better. That is why he believed that righteous people are those who should endeavor in political activities to promote change.

Political activism is the steppingstone to achieve social change. Martin Luther King utilized political activism as a tool to promote civil rights for African Americans. His work ended up paying off when Lyndon Johnson signed into law the Civil Rights Act of 1964, which granted us, the right to vote and many economic opportunities. Political power, for my father, was the way to be emancipated and to promote the most urgent needs for Blacks. A corrupt soul cannot do politics because it will harm the general welfare of the people. Only the righteous man must have that privilege. Sometimes, my father's philosophy of politics reminds me of that of Plato in his book *The Republic* which was the concept of the "philosopher king." For those who may not be familiar with that concept, the "philosopher king" concept is a principle in which Plato argued that the philosopher king is a ruler who possesses both a love of wisdom, as well as intelligence, reliability, and a willingness to live a simple life. In a nutshell, the philosopher king is a man who is highly intellectually astute and yet lives a simple life among the people that he serves. My father saw the role of the political leader that way. The political leader, for my father, should be a man who prioritizes the needs of the community over his own needs or personal interests. My run for office, is in part due to my father. I believe that if my father had the means to run for political office, he would have done it. He was extremely attached to his community. He believed that Austin deserved better. And the reason why it has been so difficult for the people of Austin to be emancipated is because the political leaders of the community were not righteous leaders. They did not implement policies that would promulgate the general welfare of the people, but policies that would amplify the power of their office. I am running to change that trend, and I am adamantly certain that my father would have been proud of me if he was alive.

I described my mother as a tough, ambitious, and self-reliant woman. This description may appear cold to some of you who will read this book, but she was, in fact, a compassionate individual who taught me how a successful man must always give back; giving back to his community, and to the people who have uplifted him. There is no point in acquiring that much wealth, that much success, power, and notoriety for yourself if you are not able to give back to those who have contributed to your success. This is the philosophy of my mother and she reminded me that concept before she passed away.

In addition to the death of my parents, I also lost three of my siblings. My older sister and two of my older brothers passed away in 2014, 2018 and 2019 respectively. Each of these losses has deeply moved me emotionally and mentally. Losing someone you love is always a predicamental situation to cope with. Of course, we have to live through it, but can we get passed it? One thing I am unquestionably certain about, is that the difficulties of life strengthen us to overcome challenges.

Life itself is a perpetual fight. From the minute we are born, we are committed to fight in order to survive. Nothing comes easy, everything we do requires a certain degree of effort and commitments, even the things that may appear easy to us still demand some efforts in order to be completed. I believe that the issues or obstacles that occur in our lives are meant to strengthen us, to make us a better person, to give a better version of ourselves. I am now a man because I confronted myself on the issues that needed to be addressed. I overcome the most pernicious hardships of my existence. Today, I feel, more than ever, ready to take on new challenges. I am ready to fight in order to improve the lives of the most vulnerable members of our district. I am committed to help them thrive. I cannot guarantee that the lives of everyone will be perfect, but I can promise to fight to the best of my abilities to improve the living conditions of everyone.

CHAPTER THREE

INTELLECTUAL AWAKENING

My intellectual awakening has been an interesting journey. Like most African Americans, I started as a conventional Democrat. When I was ideologically leaning toward the Democratic Party, I did not have a clear understanding of the fundamental political ideologies that determine American politics.

I grew up without questioning the fundamental concept of each ideology. I was told that the Republican Party was the party of old white people. A party that did not care for minorities, a party that never understood the struggle of Black people, and a party that was only concerned with promoting useless wars abroad and make the rich richer. On the other hand, I was told to believe that the Democratic Party is the political party that has the interest of minorities, especially that of black people, at heart. I was told that the Democratic Party is the political party that was concerned with social justice and political rights for minorities. I was told that Lyndon Johnson was one of the best U.S. presidents to ever rule the United States despite the debacle of the Vietnam War, because he was the one who granted Black people the right to vote when no other president dared to promote our emancipation. I was told that the Democratic Party is the party that cared about poverty and wants to fix it. In short, I was told many things when I was younger about both parties in my youth. And I used to deeply believe that these unsubstantiated statements and false beliefs were unconditionally true and could not unchallenged. As I grew up and became more mature, especially when I started to run my business, what I used to believe about politics showed to actually be not true. Let's me now examine what I mean here. When I started running my insurance and truck companies, I realized two important things: first, that the Democratic Party was never on my side; second, the Democratic Party and the Republican Party, are both two sides of the same coin that do not benefit the life of the layman.

Let me now develop what I mean in my first argument when I asseverated that the Democratic Party was never on my side. Indeed, the Democratic was not. Let me remind all of you that, between the two parties, the Democratic Party was the party that always promulgated slavery. Andrew Jackson and James Polk were both in favor of slavery. They believed that slavery was a sustainable economic system to determine growth. The moral question of arbitrarily violating the dignity of another human being on a daily basis, was clearly not a single inch of concern to them. Moreover, Andrew Johnson, the Vice President of Abraham Lincoln was a Democrat who was utterly opposed to the abolition of slavery. He saw the abolition of slavery as the collapse of the south's economy as well as the dissolution of their autonomy vis-à-vis the federal government. For Andrew Johnson, we, Black people, were subhuman. We did not deserve to live, and we were only meant to be considered as properties. Woodrow Wilson was also a progressive racist politician who relied on the black vote to acquire political power in 1912. Then, once he became president, he passed policies to relegate Blacks as second-class citizens. I could go on and on about every single Democrat president; the central point of my thought here is that the Democratic Party has been hypocritical towards minorities, especially to Blacks. One cold fact has to be stated here: the Black community is the poorest of all communities that encapsulate the national population. I did not want to use empirical evidence here, but I have to in order to demonstrate that I am not making any exaggeration. Figure 1, as you see below, illustrates the rate of poverty by race from 1974 to 2011.

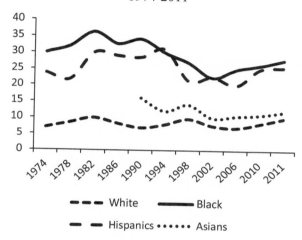

Persons in poverty by Race/Ethnicty from 1974-2011

Figure 1. Source: Pew Research Center/U.S. Census Bureau Historical Poverty Statistics. Note: For 2002-2011, whites, blacks and Asians include only persons who reported a single race; for 2001 and earlier years, respondents (including those who may be of more than one race) were allowed to report only one race group. Blacks and Asians include Hispanics for all years. Asians include Pacific Islanders prior to 2002. Data for Asians not available prior to 1987. Native Americans and other groups not shown.

There are many reasons that are at the origins of our poverty, and the welfare state is one of these deep-seated causes. Since Lyndon Johnson gave us our political rights, we however lost our economic rights. The welfare state created the low-income neighborhoods that we know through the creation of subsidized public housing, it increased the crime rate in our community, which led to a higher rate of poverty. The liberal policies of the welfare state, as I have aforementioned in the previous chapters, have destroyed the Black family unit. Moreover, as a businessowner, I was heavily taxed when Democrat administrations ran the district than Republicans. Obamacare did not make things better. It was, for the fact of the matter, the cherry on top of the cake. More money was taken away from me and my family. It did not make sense to me. If the Democratic Party claims to be the party that wants to help the poor and the most vulnerable, then it should increase our purchasing power instead of decreasing it. Common sense speaks here. No need for a doctorate in economics or a J.D. to understand this. More taxes mean less money for us to save; therefore, low incentives to invest. The Democratic Party has always favored higher taxes under the argument that "it is to invest in social programs to help the poor"; but those social programs designed to help the poor hurts them more and benefit the middle-class. The transfer of income under the guise of wealth redistribution does not benefit the poor but mostly the middle-class; a social class that is doing economically self-sufficient.

This is when my intellectual awakening came through. I realized that I was voting and vouching for a party to rob me and my family. The business taxes, in addition to Obamacare, that I was paying to the local government as well as to the state government were astronomical. Ramona and I were paying more, and we were benefitting less from it. All of our hard-earned money was automatically expropriated by the Government of Illinois and Chicago government.

Secondly, I realized that the Republican Party was no different than the Democratic Party. It operates the same way as the Democratic Party. The only difference between the two is that they just use different methods to achieve the same end. What I sincerely realized about both parties is that the Democratic Party uses morality to enforce state power while the Republican Party uses state power to enforce morality. Let me give you a concrete example of what I mean here. The Democratic Party will claim that it is the role of the government to redistribute the wealth in order to alleviate poverty while the Republican Party will claim that abortion should be criminalized because it is murder and murder is immoral. Calling for the government to redistribute the wealth in order to alleviate poverty is to clearly use morality as the justification for the use of the coercive powers of the state upon an issue that it is not supposed to be involved in. The wealth could be redistributed by other means, notably private charity, instead of calling for government action to do so and create more inequalities than there already are. And to claim that abortion must be criminalized because it is murder, is to use the coercive powers of the state to enforce a moral and religious principle that is supposed to remain in the private realm. It is not the role of the state to decide what is morally acceptable from what is not. Moral beliefs, like religious beliefs, are a matter of personal choice. The government has no power to decide upon the moral and religious values of an individual. Whether abortion is murder or not, this is not the topic of the day in this book. My point was to simply emphasize on how both parties manipulate the use of state power to achieve their ends.

It is exactly because both parties are hypocritical that I chose to go a third way. I deliberately chose to become a libertarian because it is the ideology that respects the dignity of the individual and fights for people to secure their rights. My intellectual awakening opened my eyes about the fact that there was an alternative to these two parties that bring nothing to the struggle of the layman.

The libertarian ideology is in accordance with my political beliefs and my philosophy. I have been disappointed with both parties as they benefited nobody but themselves. When we use the words "free society"; we, in fact, mean a society wherein the citizen is free to do whatever pleases him under the rule of law. If the citizen is free to do whatever pleases him under the rule of law, it subsequently suggests that the ability of the government to restrain the citizen's liberty is limited. It is a logical fallacy to believe that an individual could be considered free in a society whereby the government exerts significant influence and authority over our daily activities. Even the Republican Party, which is in theory, in favor of limited government and individual rights; cherry-picks what fits its agenda.

The Republican Party has deliberately encroached upon the rights of people on social issues in the name of upholding moral values. But my question is, if the state is an organization of legal institutions ruled by men, knowing that all men by nature are sinners; then who are these men (the rulers of the state) to decide upon what moral values to uphold and which ones should be disregarded? If all men are sinners, then no man has the moral authority to decide how another man should live his life. The Republican Party in some states has implemented punitive laws in order to uphold some sort of moral code. I believe this is a clear infringement upon individual rights, and the Republican Party has been unmistakably violating its own principles when it fits it. Neither party promotes the freedom of the individual. Both parties promote the expansion of the powers of government, but they only do it differently to achieve the same ends. My political philosophy is no longer on the same page with both parties.

My intellectual awakening made me realize that our political system is inherently flawed. Today, politics has become purely corporatism. Both, the Democratic Party and the Republican Party are the two giant corporations that dominate the political market the same way the "Big Four" (Amazon, Google, Facebook, and Apple) are dominating the tech industry. The United States political system has many political parties. I do not want to exaggerate, but I think we have over a hundred political parties. Yet, because of the two-party system we have, the other political parties are basically irrelevant in the political market. If an individual wants to run for a national political office such as U.S. Congress or the U.S. Senate, he must run either as a Democrat or as Republican, in order to increase his chances to win. For example, Bernie Sanders is a member of the Democratic Socialist Party of America (DSPA). But as he is running for President of the United States in a political duopoly, he had to run as a Democrat if he wants to increase his chances of being President.

Since the national population is politically accustomed to the duopolistic system that we have in America, then most people will be reluctant to vote for a candidate that is not part of the two parties. I believe in perfect competition. To me, perfect competition means letting the small guy competing as well; to giving him his chance to show what he worth. The two-party system shall be dismantled, in my humble opinion. It shall be dismantled and dissolved in order to give way to a multi-party system where all political parties can fully compete in the political market. The Libertarian Party is the third largest party of the country. However, because of this duopolistic system, the Libertarian Party cannot fully exercise the fullness of its electoral potential. We are all subjected to abide by the rules of the Democratic Party and the Republican Party.

Since my intellectual awakening has taken place, I believe to have ideologically and politically matured. I founded my purpose; and my political mission; and I am now utterly committed to promote liberty and to spread all around the state of Illinois.

CHAPTER FOUR

LOVE FOR LIBERTY

Being a libertarian is sometimes not easy. You are mocked, ridiculed, and scorned by those who believe in mainstream politics. They usually say that libertarians are too dogmatic, too theoretical, too principled, too ideologically naïve, and too unconcerned with poverty. Libertarians are scorned by mainstream politics for their inability to win a significant election whether it is at the local, state, or federal level.

The problem is not on the side of the libertarians, but rather on the side of mainstream politics. The problem with mainstream politics is that it is willing to violate its ideological principles if the political situation is not favorable to their agenda. I am fully aware that in politics, we need to compromise constantly, and that we cannot always apply our ideology in every single issue. Yet, I believe that even if compromising on policy is important in order to get things done, I do not believe however that principles shall be compromised. If ideologies are meant to be violated or encroached on a regular basis, then there is no point for a political party to exist in the first place. A political party exists, first and foremost, because it has an ideological basis. However, if for example, a party claims to support limited government and individual rights, but implements a set of policies that increases government power over the rights of the citizens, then that party is not a political party but simply a corporation that seeks to make profit by all means rather than remaining faithful to its ideological guidelines.

I love liberty. I believe that there is nothing better than liberty. In fact, the opposition of liberty is serfdom, slavery, bondage, servitude, and vassalage. Above all else, liberty is the absence of coercion. It is important to fathom that the achievements that have happened in the world, have not happened through government action. On the contrary, they have occurred by individual action. For example, Steve Jobs has improved human activity through the creation of Apple device, the Wright brothers had facilitated human ability to travel long distance from point A to point B through airplanes; Willis Carrier found a way to improve the conduct of human activities during times of hot weather through the creation of air conditioning; Alexander Graham Bell is today credited for having invented the telephone, which improved our ability to communicate with one another and ameliorated the methods of communication between two individuals who would not be present at the same place and at the same time. I can give a thousand more examples to substantiate my point. That being said, governments have never created something substantive that has significantly improved the lives of people for the better. These people I just mentioned in these examples, were able to achieve what they achieved because they were free to do so. Government did not subvert them to act a certain way. Government would have not been able to create any of these items because it lacks the information necessary to determine the quantity and the method to produce such items.

Freedom enables the individual to create and to undertake. Moreover, freedom enables the individual to help his fellow man. The societies that are the most advanced today are those that have a higher degree of freedom. Evidently, those on the Left always use Scandinavia as an example to justify their political beliefs, the expansion of the welfare state and the rise of socialism in the United States; but Scandinavia, at the end of the day, is not a socialistic society. Their economic system is clearly based upon a capitalistic model because their access to private property is significantly high. It is higher than most countries on the planet. It signifies that there is a higher degree of freedom in Scandinavia than in most developed countries. For example, figure 2 shows here economic freedom index of Sweden from 1995 to 2019. According to the standards of the Economic Freedom Index of the Heritage Foundation, a country is considered to be free if its scores above 60 percent. The economic trend of Sweden is clearly above that standard.

Figure 2. Source: Economic Freedom Index of the Heritage Foundation

If Sweden and the majority of Scandinavian countries did not value freedom as the basis of their economic systems, they would have not been as developed. Moreover, Scandinavian countries produced more billionaires than the United States or the United Kingdom. If private property was not accessible in Scandinavia, then some individuals would have not been able to become billionaires. If Scandinavian countries were truly socialist, then nobody would have become a billionaire. Expect the members of the governments in each Scandinavian country.

One who believes in freedom shall believe in the freedom of businesses to operate freely; which means that the minimum wage is a coercive method to compel businesses to pay their employees. As a businessowner myself, the augmentation of the minimum wage prevented me from paying my employees the wage that reflects their true skills. By compelling me to pay an employee a wage that does not reflect his skills, the state takes my freedom to decide how to run my own business while the right to undertake explicitly means the right to decide how the owner of the means of production will utilize the resources he possesses to increase his capital.

Liberty is clearly at stake in the state of Illinois. Overtime, the state of Illinois has become a "blue" state. Anyone who reads this book knows what I mean by blue. Most Illinoisans, and particularly Chicagoans, are supporters and voters of the Democratic Party. Our current governor, J.B. Pritzker sought to implement a law that will change our tax system from a flat income tax system to a progressive income tax system. Most Illinoisans believe that the state of Illinois has a bigger role to play in the life of our citizenry. Such attitude drastically restrains our freedom. I must admit that it is going to be hard to bring back the foundational precepts of liberty in Illinois. The American citizen in general is culturally and politically accustomed to believing that the federal government, the state government, and local government have a role of play. I am not saying that government, in general, has no role to play at all. In fact, it does, but its role is to only protect the rights of the citizens and to provide the infrastructures necessary to expand access to the market. In the next chapter I will further develop this portion of my argument to a greater extent. But my main point is to reiterate that the role of government is to protect the rights of the citizen, and to deliver the infrastructures required to create economic growth.

The role of the government is not to provide goods and services to the citizenry such as education, health, or transportations to the general population. These kinds of goods could be supplied by the market more efficiently, in my opinion. I deeply believe that if such goods were supplied by private means, output would be, either way, higher than it is today. Today, in Austin (where I am from), public schools are run terribly mainly because the administrators are not free since they work for the government. Our education system is subjected to the power of the state to a greater extent that it is very scary. I believe that the most efficient way to bring liberty to the state of Illinois, is by educating the people about the history of this country and the history of the U.S. Constitution. Most of us do not really understand the Constitution of our country, and without this important comprehension of the Constitution of our country, we cannot thoroughly fathom what liberty is about and what our Founding Fathers have bequeathed us.

The power of government ought to be restrained to its smallest scope possible. Government exists because we are not angels, as James Madison would say. If we were angels, we would not need government. A government is necessary, but it must be substantially limited solely to protect our constitutional rights and to grant our access to private property. A government does not exist to impose upon us some conditionalities which would compromise our freedom for security. If we forsake our freedom for security, we then become subjects of the state. It suggests that, as subjects of the state, we can only execute what the state tells us to do. As subjects of the state, we lose our ability to legitimately question the action of government. The Soviets were subjects of their government, and that is why they could not raise questions against their government or rebel against it if their government's action became illegitimate. In America, freedom is not a privilege, it is a right. It is a God-given right. It is a right that precedes political authority. My goal, as future State Representative of District 78, is to propose legislations to the state legislature that which will ensure that the original purpose of government is restored so that the layman could have a greater freedom.

Part Two

THE POLITICAL
CANDIDATE

CHAPTER FIVE

LOWER TAXES

"Lower Taxes." These two words are the basis of the economic policy of the Republican Party as well as that of the Libertarian Party. Ronald Reagan is widely adulated by millions of Americans in general, and by Republicans in particular, who have avowed that he is their hero. Ronald Reagan is mainly considered as a hero for the American Right because his economic policy principally focused on lowering taxes for businesses, corporation, the upper and the middle-class. In short, the lower-taxes policy of Reagan stimulated economic growth in the 1980s after the brief recession at the

56

commencement of his presidency. Consequently, lowering taxes is an essential feature of any economic policy. It is, as a matter of fact, one of the three key elements of my platform for the general election of 2020.

My economic policy is principally embedded in lowering taxes because I believe that lowering taxes creates economic growth. District 78 does need economic growth. The subsequent figure I am about to illustrate is the data that shows how the median income in Austin has shrunk from 2010 to 2017. The data shows that the median household income in Austin shrunk from $36,562 in 2010 to $32,843 in 2017.

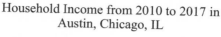

Household Income from 2010 to 2017 in
Austin, Chicago, IL

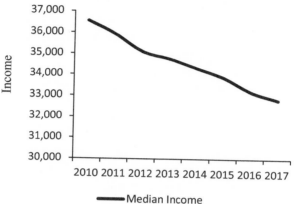

Figure 3. Source: 2006-2010 and 2013-2017 American Community
Survey five-year estimates.

The main reason why income has shrunk in Austin is because of the tax code that Camille Lilly has passed in the Legislature since she has been in office. The truth of the matter is that, when we increase taxes, income eventually decrease because the government takes a substantial portion of our income to spend on various programs that

58

sometimes do not benefit the community. For example, our education system remains relatively poor in terms of academic performance. What is the government doing with our money? What has Camille Lilly been doing with the money of the Illinoisans? She has been in office since 2010, and since then the people of District 78 are making less.

My plan to lowering taxes has only one purpose: To increase the purchasing power of the people of District 78. More money in their pockets means more money to spend. It also means more investment could be made in order to increase growth in our community. More money in their pocket will also help the people of District 78 planning their budget accordingly, which means that they can also save more by having more in their pocket. Yet, the ability to spend is a personal trend which each citizen knows how much he or she can afford. Yet my tax plan can be divided in three substantive points: (1) property tax, (2) income tax, and (3) sales taxes. I seek to reduce taxes in each of these of these points.

(1) Property taxes

The state of Illinois has one of the highest property taxes in the country. It is for this very main reason that a lot of people have fled the state of Illinois for the southern states. Property taxes are astronomically high, and they are a predicament in the income of Illinois resident. In fact, property taxes take about two-third of our paychecks. Figure 4 shows my point; how property tax has outpaced income growth in Illinois in the past three decades.

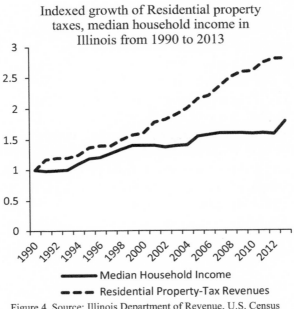

Figure 4. Source: Illinois Department of Revenue, U.S. Census Bureau, Illinois Policy Institute

By reducing property tax rates, we will be able to adjust to the index between median household and residential property-tax revenues.

(2) Income taxes

As I have elucidated in the previous chapter, the state of Illinois has a flat income tax system. However, the tax rate of our income tax code is drastically high as well. This is another reason why many people are leaving the State of Illinois. Worst, Governor Pritzker wants to transition from a flat income tax to a progressive income tax. There are, however, empirical evidence which substantiate that states with a progressive income tax, we have a lower economic productivity. Figure 5 does once again prove my point that having a progressive income tax, will hurt the Illinois economy.

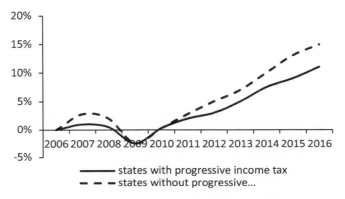

Figure 5. Source: Bureau of Economic Analysis, Illinois Policy Institute

I believe that, like the property tax rate, the income tax rate shall be reduced while keeping the same flat income tax system. A flat income tax system, in my humble opinion, is the surest, the most adequate, and the most democratic form of taxation because everybody pays the same tax rate regardless of income made. No one is privileged, and no one is punished either for making more income than others. A progressive income tax would be a punitive way to express resentment toward those who have worked hard to earn their money. I do not believe that it is morally nor economically fair to tax more those who earn more. True equality, once again in my humble opinion, is to put everybody on the same standard and to treat them equally according to those standards. The flat income tax system perfectly reflects that equality.

(3) Sale taxes

Our state has also one of the highest sales taxes in the nation. At least I thank the Lord that our sales taxes are not as high as those in Washington, D.C., New York or California. Nonetheless, I believe that our sale taxes could be further reduced because it will help our economic producing more goods and services for the people of Illinois. Once again, let me reiterate that more taxes mean more power to the state and less power to the consumer. It should be the other way around. It should be more power to the consumer and less power to the state. Taxation is the system by which the state exerts a direct and coercive control over the citizenry. Consequently, this ability of the state to exercise such authority over the citizenry shall be contained. The best method to contain it is to reduce its rates.

Cutting taxes will help businesses flourishing. Less taxes for businesses mean that they can make more profit, and therefore they can hire more people. Businesses are willing to settle into an area where they will not have to pay an excessive rate of taxes. Less taxes lead to economic productivity. The lower taxes are, the more people would want to work because they know that they will earn more in their paycheck during the pay-cycle. In fact, it is an incentive for workers to double their productivity, and it is a great opportunity for firms to maximize profit. Everybody wins

The maximization of profit is what leads to the creation and the accumulation of capital. Low taxes will enable businesses to invest in their capital stock. This investment in capital stock will create new opportunity to expand upon their capital, which will lead to more accumulation. More taxes lead to an increase in unemployment because businesses are compelled to pay to the states, in taxes, most of the profits they have made from their sales. The problem is that, if a business pays the state most of the profit it has made from its sales, then how is it going to compensate its employees? Of course, corporations can afford paying their employees no matter the tax burden imposed upon them. But what about the little guy? What about the small business that is at the start-up level and is trying to generate profit and reinvest that profit in its capital stock in order to satisfy the needs of the community? Lowering taxes will considerably help small businesses to expand on their productivity and this expansion will stimulate growth.

I pledge to the people of District 78 to not increase a single digit of their tax rate but to reduce it so that everyone can benefit from it and prosper. My goal is to see my district harvesting the fruit of its hard labor. I want the layman to feel confident that he lives in a district where his elected state representative has not abandoned him. I want the layman to believe that the solution to improve his condition, is not to rely on a politician that will increase his taxes but one that will lower his taxes so that he could start a business on his own. I believe that lowering taxes will help the most marginalized members of our community to have faith again in the American Dream. Anything is possible to the individual who deeply and stubbornly holds on to his dream. I want to facilitate this process for everyone. More economic opportunities lead to less crime and safer streets.

CHAPTER SIX

ECONOMIC DEVELOPMENT

The economic development of the District 78 is the second core element of my campaign. I believe that the state has a role to play in promoting the economic development of the District. The economic development of a region is a very important factor for growth's stimulation. I believe that District 78 has a tremendous potential to become one of the most productive and flourishing places in Illinois for economic prosperity. My plan to promote the economic development of District 78 consists of four main substantive points: (1) Investing in the infrastructures to help promoting economic growth; (2) creating the conditions to increase employment in the private sector; (3) investing in the education system to improve the educational attainment of the people of District 78; and (4) cut spending for useless government programs. I believe that a diligent implementation of each of these elements of the plan will lead to a greater outcome for the people of District 78.

(1) Investment in infrastructures

It is important to remind the reader two important points that I aforementioned throughout this book. First, that government is needed in certain realms because the market cannot provide every single thing to the general population. Second, that the role of the government though shall be limited only in providing the infrastructures necessary to facilitate the access of the layman to the market process. Apart from these two points, the government has no other substantive role to play in economic and social activities.

Let me reiterate once again that it is not the role of the government; whether it is the federal government, the state government, or the local government; to control the economic activities of the ordinary man. One way for government to control the economic activity of the ordinary man is by controlling the price system. If the government controls the price system, it therefore controls the mechanism of supply and demand. Yet this supply-and-demand mechanism it may control though is an artificial mechanism; not a natural one. The price system is not meant to be controlled by the political process but by the market process, which means that prices are and should be determined by the needs and wants of consumers, not that of bureaucrats. The role of government is to invest in the infrastructures necessary to facilitate the access to the market for the layman. Let me give you an example. In the 1870s, which is the decade after slavery was abolished in the United States, immigration in the United States also surged. Many Europeans immigrated to the United States for economic opportunities. The federal government gave a substantial amount of lands to these European immigrants to engage in their agricultural and farming activities while the newly freed slaves had absolutely nothing to rely on in order to engage in economic activities. The federal government had deprived the newly freed slaves of these same economic opportunities that it has granted to the white European immigrants. These lands provided to the European immigrants were not subsidized by the federal government.

The point here was to epitomize how government provides the infrastructures to the ordinary man in order for him to engage in the market process. The state government has the duty provide the infrastructures to the layman in order to help him engage in the market process. That is why I believe that the state shall invest in infrastructures. The more we invest in our infrastructures, the easier it will be the for layman to improve his economic activities as well as his life condition.

(2) Increase Employment in the Private Sector

The improvement of employment in Austin, and within the rest of the district, is my absolute priority to promote the economic development of the district. I am going to illustrate here an important table which assesses the employment condition in Austin.

EMPLOYMENT STATUS 2013-2017

	Austin County (Percent)
In Labor Force	55.4
Employed	84.6
Unemployed	15.4
Not in Labor Force	44.6

Table 1. Source: 2013-2017 American Community Survey five-year estimates. Note: This table does not include employed population in the Armed Forces.

Although there are more people employed in the labor force than unemployed, I believe that we can do better. 15.4 of unemployment is a considerably high number when we assess unemployment rate. The natural rate of unemployment in the United States is considered to be around 4.5 percent to 5 percent according to the Bureau of Labor Statistics. When unemployment rates reach the double-digits, it becomes an alarming situation to cope with. Consequently, 15.4 percent of unemployment is an alarming situation. The most effective way, in my humble opinion, to reduce unemployment in Austin and in District 78, is for the local government to work with the private industries in creating new jobs in the private sector. For the private sector to create new jobs, taxes must be lowered and access to private property shall be widened. It means that the rules and regulations that are imposed upon the creation of a business must be loosened in order to give to the layman the chance to create something for himself, and to expand upon it.

There is 44.6 percent of the people in Austin who are not in the labor force. This is about half of the community that is not engaged in any form of economic activity. This percentage must be further reduced by promoting the creation of more jobs in the digital realm, in the service realm, and in the manufacturing realm. The investment in infrastructures will logically create economic opportunities for the local entrepreneurs of the communities; and these opportunities will subsequently create more jobs because there are more entrepreneurs who will be registering their business entity with the State Department of Illinois. Furthermore, the creation of economic opportunities will attract other investors and companies to wanting to settle in Austin. That will be a great opportunity to increase employment. It will certainly lift hundreds, and even thousands of people out of poverty. I am confident that what is needed to be done, is for the government to step back from the economic activities of District 78. We shall trust the individuals to make their own decisions. Men will always make mistakes. That is why we are, first, and foremost, individuals. But I do not believe that the state can run the lives of the citizens better than they can run their own lives. I do not believe that it is the role of the State of Illinois to create jobs in the public sector for Illinoisan as well as for the people of District 78. Jobs in the public sector may be necessary, but they are highly inefficient because it strips away the competition for higher aims. Those who work in the public sector have these jobs for life. There are not subjected to the threat of being terminated. It sure gives them security, but at the same time, it attenuates their motivation to seek higher aims professionally while in the private sector, the fear of being professionally terminated incentivizes the worker to produce more, and therefore to augment his own efficiency and dexterity.

(3) Improving our Educational System

Nelson Mandela used to asseverate that education is the most powerful weapon which we can use to change the world. Undeniably, Madiba was right. Education is an important tool for promoting economic and social growth.

However, many people do not rely on education as the tool to which they could achieve their ends. Many people see education as a chore and as a flaw because they believe that it is an investment that does not necessarily reward. I could not entirely disagree with their assessment. Conversely, education is important because it is the foundational tool that enables the economic development of a society. For example, Japan is one of the most advanced countries on earth despite not having a single natural resource to rely on in order to develop their economy. The reason why Japan is so developed and economically self-sufficient is because it has invested in its people through education. No one can contest that Japan has far more physicists, computer scientists, doctors, and a great number of scientists than most developed nations. This fact is undeniable. If the Japanese did not value education as the main tool for promoting economic and social growth, Japan would have been considered as a low-income country.

Education plays an important role in a society whether it is at the macro or micro level because a population that has a higher rate of literacy will deliver a higher productivity and output. Most of the human activities that enable the progress of the human condition are endeavors that require intellectual and analytical skills. For example, we all use smartphones for many different reasons other than calling and sending text messages. Yet the design and manufacturing of such gadgets require a substantial application of analytical skills; mainly mathematical skills; for the smartphone to function properly. If there were no mathematicians to apply their knowledge upon the manufacturing of these gadgets, smartphones would have not existed today, and it would have been ten times harder for us to complete many of our daily tasks that demand the application of certain information. What is important to understand about education is that it requires patience before it pays off. The more a community is educated, the more opportunities arise within its reach. Table 2 shows the educational attainment in Austin from 2010 to 2017.

EDUCATIONAL ATTAINMENT, 2010-2017

	2010(%)	2017(%)
Less than High School Graduate	25.0	21.3
High School Graduate or Equivalency	34.6	35.1
Some College, No Degree	21.7	22.1
Associate Degree	7.8	7.5
Bachelor's Degree	7.2	9.3
Graduate Degree	3.6	4.9

Table 2. Source: 2006-2010 and 2013-2017 American Community Survey five-year estimates

These results are not that great to be quite frank. I believe that the best way to improve our education system is to empower private means to run our schools. In other words, I believe that government-owned schools should transition into charter schools. According to a study conducted by the Illinois Department of Education, which evaluated the performances of government-owned schools and charter schools, charter schools have better performances than traditional public schools. Government-owned schools perform significantly less than charter schools because these schools are officiated by the government. Teachers and staff have no incentives to improve the academic performance of the students in these schools because no matter what happens, these teachers will still earn their salary and will still keep their jobs while the future of these children is compromised. Furthermore, government-owned schools in low-income neighborhoods are poorly maintained, which set students for failure and for unemployment. In order to tackle this issue, it is important to implement new policies that will pave the way for an improvement in the student's academic performances. In charter schools, the role of the government will not be to impose a curriculum upon the method whereby the school shall be administered, but only to supply the tools that students need in order to improve their performance. Charter schools generally perform better than government-owned schools because they are privately managed although they are subsidized by the state. The political war that is currently occurring in our education system is that the government refuses to subsidize an entity that it cannot control. It resents giving money to schools upon which it cannot impose its curriculum. It has never been the role of the state to educate children. The education of a child is the responsibility of parents. By promoting charter schools, we give the ability to parents to choose where they want and how they want their children to be educated. Lastly, I believe that a voucher system will be a good and effective method to improve the academic performances of students from low-income neighborhoods.

(4) Cut Spending on Useless Government Programs

It is undeniable that the welfare state exists for a reason. Yet it has not done the job it was supposed to do. Since the welfare exists, whether it is at the federal or state level, it has not benefited the most marginalized members of society. The State of Illinois has a dozen of welfare programs such as the Illinois Weatherization Assistance Program, the Illinois Summer Food Service, the Illinois Temporary Assistance for Needy Families (TANF), and the Illinois Food Stamps

Program. These programs, despite their genuine intentions, do not improve the living conditions of its recipients nor that it increases their living standards. Instead, they are dependent on these programs, which take away their incentives to become responsibility for their own lives.

According to a study conducted by the Cato Institute and the Illinois Policy Institute, an Illinois family of one mother and two children receiving TANF; Medicaid; food stamps, public housing; utility assistance; and free commodities; would have a benefits package with $19,442 per year. How do we expect the individual to be responsible for himself if that person receives all these benefits from the taxpayer? I fully comprehend that life is tough sometimes and it is not easy for everybody to get back on their feet economically. However, I do not believe that it is by assisting the individual through government means, in every possible way that his condition will improve. Of course, some people do need help. This is undeniable. Yet, instead of using the political process to achieve these goals, why not rely on the market means such as private charity to fulfill these ends? The truth of the matter is that it is not fair for some people to live at the expenses of others. These programs cost too much to the taxpayers. This money we spend on these programs could be invested in more profitable ventures such as new infrastructures (the creation of new hospitals, schools, and public transportations) or into educational programs that will help young adults to improve their professional condition. It is time to cut spending in these programs. Let's use our money wisely, let's invest in activities that will thoroughly improve the lives of the Illinoisans. Not to suffocate them economically.

CHAPTER SEVEN

SAFER STREETS

I come from a neighborhood that is not safe. I must admit it. Gun violence is a serious conundrum in my community. It greatly pains me to see young black kids involving themselves in gang violence and drug issues because they have no paternal guidance at home to explain to them why some actions shall not be performed and what consequences these actions could potentially lead to.

Violence in Austin and in other neighborhoods in the district, has increased during the recent years. It has scared me personally; it has scared my wife as well. We raised our children insofar as they will not fall for gang violence and drug consumption. When we observe the American legal system, especially the criminal justice system; it has been used as a tool; sometimes as a punitive tool against African Americans to an extent. Make no mistake, I am not saying that the criminal justice system is utterly unfair. Not at all. We have one of the best criminal justice systems that the free world has ever produced. Our system of due process is considerably unmatched compared to that of European countries. Nevertheless, it is important and fair to say that our criminal justice system has not been entirely fair to all of its citizens. Empirical evidence has shown that the criminal justice system has mainly been, since its creation, an adversarial system for African Americans. According to a study conducted by the NAACP, in 2014, African Americans alone, constituted 2.3 million, or 34 percent of the total 6.8 million correctional population. Evidently, African Americans are not, by the numbers, the most incarcerated in the American prisons on the scale of the national population; but among all the minority populations, we are indeed the most incarcerated. Table 3 shows the last updated allocation of inmates by race according to the Federal Bureau of Prisons. Blacks represent 37.5 percent of inmates while whites represent 58.6 percent.

INMATE RACE

Race	#of Inmates	% of Inmates
Asian	2,681	1.5%
Black	65,678	37.5%
Native American	4,109	2.3%
White	102,570	58.6%

Table 3. Source: Federal Bureau of Prisons, statistics based on prior month's (February) data—last updated; Saturday, 7 2020.

Even though there are more whites incarcerated than blacks, as I have said, this is so because whites represent the majority of the national population. Therefore, it is logical that there are more whites incarcerated than blacks. The same mechanism goes for welfare. There are more whites on welfare than blacks because there are more whites than blacks on the population basis. But, one fact remains constant, which is that blacks are twice likely to go to be arrested and go to jail than whites for petty crimes. The incarceration of a person leads to a social prison. As I said it in the first chapter of this book, a person with a criminal record is less likely to obtain a job, or rent an apartment, and is more likely to remain in long-term poverty.

In order to make our streets safer in the district, I propose two substantive plans. First, I propose that my prospective colleagues change the penal laws by decriminalizing crimes that should not be rigorously enforced. In my eyes, to rigorously enforcing the law upon a petty crime means that it does not have the intent to protect the safety of the residents of the community but to fill up prisons' quotas. Therefore, the decriminalization of petty crimes is a top priority in my legislative agenda. Safer streets imply building a safe and healthy relationship between the community and the police. The police must be held accountable when it abuses its power through the use of excessive force over the citizenry and the citizenry must also be held accountable when it does not obey the law.

The second measure I propose is the reeducation of prisoners. The reader may ask himself or herself, "what has reeducating the prisoner have to do with safer streets?" Well, there is a direct correlation between these two variables. I believe that prisoners shall be reeducated because they can become once again an asset for society's progress. I believe that if we offer a vocational training to inmates, it will revitalize their sense of purpose as well as it will empower them with a sum of skillset that they could use on the labor market once they are rehabilitated into civil society. I believe that everyone deserves a second chance unless that person has been sentenced to life imprisonment without parole. The inmate who has been rehabilitated in the streets with a vocational education will seek to maximize the utility of what he owns, which is the skillset he has acquired while learning vocational training in prison. Logically, that person will no longer become a flight risk for the community but simply an individual who is seeking social redemption. Education and entrepreneurship are the two substantial incentives that will surely keep our streets safe. These two incentives will especially protect our youth from falling into gang violence and drugs. Safer streets lead to a better economic development, better economic growth, and to a substantive capital accumulation.

It important to understand that economic development can happen within a place or a region that is economically poor. That is no problem. But it cannot happen within a place or a region that is not safe. Investors will be reluctant to put their money into an instable place because they have no guarantee to have the return of their investment. That is why, stability and safety are a priority to ensure economic development in a low-income neighborhood like Austin. Austin can definitely become a place of economic development, growth, and investment if we implement the right laws and policies which will incentivize the layman to give the best of himself in order to promote the economic and social development of his community.

Made in USA - Kendallville, IN
1060958_9798626789072
03.23.2020 0824